The Pattern
of Music

BY

GEORGE SHERMAN DICKINSON

Professor of Music, Vassar College

VASSAR COLLEGE
POUGHKEEPSIE, NEW YORK
1939

CONTENTS

Citations in the text in bracketed numerals refer to the correspondingly numbered musical illustrations given in the LISTENING REPERTORY *of phonograph records*

PUBLISHED IN CELEBRATION OF
THE SEVENTY-FIFTH ANNIVERSARY
OF VASSAR COLLEGE AND IN HONOR
OF HENRY NOBLE MACCRACKEN
IN THE TWENTY-FIFTH YEAR OF
HIS PRESIDENCY

THE PATTERN OF MUSIC

MUSIC is in final essence an experience. The specific identity of a musical work lies therefore in the response of the particular individual to it; and an intrinsic, ideal identity can exist only in the optimum response which the work is capable of arousing in individuals of superior sensitivity and finely adjusted receptiveness.

This response is at the full a pervasive and deep one. It involves a direct, subtly fluctuating sensuous reaction to the stimuli of tone movement; it involves an engrossing intellectual synthesis of the cumulative relations of tones into the higher and higher coördinations of the whole; and it contains a resultant mood saturation, which develops in quality and intensity in consonance with the character of both the physical and the mental condition which the music induces. But the response to music is not a mere sum of these fractions: for music moves through the entire being of the listener with a singular power of integration. This state of response in its entirety—the musical experience itself—individualized in each work, *is* the "expression" of the music.

Contingent as music is upon realization in a living experience, the tone organism, which is the source of the experience and from the particular character of which the experience must draw its quality, may nevertheless be inspected in suspended animation. Even in such partial detachment from experience it is feasible to search for the nature of the tone relations, the effect of which upon the human organism is so potent.

The musical organism has its existence, in this abstract sense, in the unique realm of tone motion, and is in principle a body of evolving tone patterns. It is the patterned nature of the tone organism which we shall undertake to examine.

I. IDEA

PATTERNED MOTION IN ONE LINE

The primal element of all music is the TONE LINE, the distinctive mark of which is its quality of simultaneous motion in three dimensions. While the access to this motion is purely aural, figurative terms are suggestive in describing it. In such terms the tone line may be conceived as an advancing movement, composed quantitatively of up-down motion in pitch coupled with forward motion in time, and attended qualitatively by an inflecting swell-fade motion in volume.

Motion in its most precise form in the dimension of pitch may be viewed as proceeding from tone to tone by some kind of step. But however acoustically exact the relations may be intended to be, the listener supplies an intervening sensation of glide in support of the tone motion. The aggregate of a number of steps makes therefore what is in effect a moving pitch curve. The curve may be extremely simple in contour or of great complexity, depending on the total range through which it sweeps, on the distance and character of the individual moves, and on the frequency of the moves. In greater lengths the curve may trace elaborate convolutions, in the course of which narrower curves are contained within wider ones. Nor are the relations merely those of immediately successive pitches: tones several moves away, claiming importance through various forms of emphasis, may refer backward and forward to other important tones in a supercontour. Whatever the complication of the curve, it is one of compensating fluctuations, in which, by and large, movement in one direction is sooner or later approximately balanced by an opposite swing.

The tone line, in the unfolding of its pitch curve, also embodies between successive tones differences of acoustical relation, which give the impression of varying degrees of affinity. Relations conveying a comparatively closer sense of association or fusion between successive tones are consonant; those producing a greater sense of dissociation or tension are dissonant. The tone line is thus felt to be impelled by a series of strains and releases in compensating interplay.

The product, in the dimension of pitch, of such relations as these among the members of the tone line constitutes a *pitch pattern*.

It is obvious that a related succession of tones cannot be conceived as real except as it takes shape in time. To the curve of pitch motion there is therefore inextricably matched a forward motion in the dimension of time. As distinguished from pitch motion by step, this is a movement which advances by graduated flow. The time graduations, like the movements of the pitch curve, may be simple or complicated in relation, according to the similarity or difference in length of the moments of time laid off, according to the frequency with which the moves take place, and according to the manner of distribution of points of emphasis. This process likewise reveals a principle of compensation according to which greater activity at one moment tends to be recompensed sooner or later by lesser activity at another.

Motion in the dimension of time, advancing in such

relations as these, is the embodiment of a *rhythmic pattern*.

The coalesced motions of the tone line in the dimensions of pitch and time display definition of pattern, though a mechanistic one wanting in full artistic significance. But with the interpretative inflection contributed by an attendant motion in the dimension of volume, the tone line achieves aesthetic veracity. The swell-fade motion in this dimension is in character a shading, the fluctuations of which form a volume curve susceptible of inexhaustible variety of application.

Since the volume curve is entirely contingent upon the shape which it may best take for confirmation of the pitch-time pattern, it will itself assume a simple or a compound form according to the dictates of that pattern. As a reflection of the pitch-time pattern, increases and decreases of volume are likely to occur in reinforcement of movements of approach to and departure from organically important tones or areas of the tone pattern. In the rendering of such emphases an important resource of volume effect lies in the diversified application of the frequency and rate of increase or decrease of volume. In increase of volume there is a quality of pressure and in decrease one of release, which make active contribution to the sense of projection and of sustainment of motion in the tone line.

Thus, though the volume curve lacks the definitive movement possessed by pitch-time pattern, its fluctuations must nevertheless be accepted as an actual *nuance pattern,* the animating force of which is indispensable to the quality of the tone line.

Most significant of all, in the conception of the tone line, is the fact that the patterns in the several dimensions of pitch, time, and volume enhance one another, and that it is the mutuality of their relations which imparts definition to the collective motion. Through these interdependent resources of pattern, the complex of motion of the tone line exhibits manifold degrees and kinds of definition, ranging from insignificant repetitive monotone to soaring flight. Tone lines may hence be thought of as revealing inherent differences of individuality or *value*. In a large sense any tone line, however limited, may bring something of significance to the organism of the whole. More specifically, however, the tone line of relatively superior value, by virtue of which it contributes indispensably to the reasoned order of the musical design, is MELODY. An integral pattern — a unique entity, the aspects of which are pitch, rhythmic, and nuance pattern—now claims recognition, that is, *melodic pattern* itself. [52, 71, 44, 70]

MELODIC ORIENTATION

The patterned nature of melody suggests that it does not exist as a generality of motion. On the contrary, it is in essence onward-moving and directional. This signifies objectives and routes to the objectives, in a word, orientation of the motion.

Since the orienting process implies the listener's perception of relations, it can function only through a procedure which induces comparisons. But relations in the incessantly unfolding musical organism must be recognized by the listener, not computed, for only thus is that spontaneous comparison possible which the mobility of music necessitates. Hence the factors subject to comparison must within reasonable limits be knowable by the perceiver and different enough to invite recognition. It is consequently evident that melodic orientation, in accord with the three dimensions of melodic motion, must operate through appreciable pitch and time vocabularies, and with reference to a definable frame of volume. In the evolution of mu-

[5

sical art various such criteria have developed, too many and too technical in character for presentation here. But whatever the system, the principle of recognizable bases of comparison remains the *sine qua non* of melodic intelligibility. Only in a specific orientation does melodic pattern acquire character and the impulse of advance.

In the great body of civilized music the usual basis of pitch comparison is found in various vocabularies of tones, evolved by experiment, accumulated by tradition, and fixed by usage. In each of these the systematic relations of the tones to one another depend upon their mutual relation to a tone of reference, which is accorded a degree of importance through serving as a chosen point of arrival of melodic motion. Such a set of relations is a MODE (loosely, a scale). Its systematic character rests on the particular scheme of pitch relations which it contains, in most musical systems, within the acoustical frame of the octave. Its aesthetic character is a reflection of the given relations and is manifested in the individual flavor or "ethos" which pervades a melody the tones of which embody these relations. [52, 44] The "majorness" of the major mode is a familiar illustration of mode quality. [44, 70]

The further endowment of the tones of a mode, through manner of use, with relatively different degrees of energy of motion toward the tone of reference, renders a mode a hierarchy of tones, in which the chief tone is not merely a tone of reference but a focus of gravitational attraction. Motion toward the tone of reference accordingly acquires insistence, and the relatively passive tone of reference becomes an active *tonic* tone. This phenomenon is MELODIC TONALITY. [70]

The integrative force of tonality derives from certain reinforcing acoustical relations among the tones of the mode, from a melodic behavior which predicts motion toward the tonic through prominence and persistence of that tone, and from the psychological factor of will-to-attain a predicted tone objective. In the perception of tonality the listener must accept and focus upon the tone of reference if it is to exert its full function as a tonic. Furthermore, in the conviction of tonal motion the coöperation of time pattern is vital, since the sense of direction and the effect of arrival involve not merely a *where,* but also a confirming *when* in their formulation.

The tones of a given mode, however, are not necessarily the only ones which may enter into a melody conceived in that mode. Other tones, lying in intermediate relation to those of the mode proper, may join the melodic curve. Their contribution is that of diversification and enrichment of the mode vocabulary. Unless they are excessively numerous and prominent in location, they are drawn within the field of control of the tonic and serve to expand its effective area. They are called *chromatic* tones.

Other systems than those based on mode and tonality, which nevertheless afford perceivable bases of tone comparison, have appeared at various times in the history of music. Thus in the atonal styles the melodic line is oriented to points thrown into local relief within itself, rather than to a single ultimate tone of reference. Whatever the type of relation, aural familiarity on the part of the listener with the tone system underlying it is corequisite to an intelligible grasp of melodic patterns formed in the given set of terms.

A basis of time comparison among the tones of the melodic line arises from the fact that equality of emphasis in a succession is both psychologically impossible and aesthetically sterile. Some points in the tone line attract greater emphasis, others less or none at all. Such distinctions of emphasis are essential to the spontaneous perception of time relation. Two general forms of distribution of emphasis, one irregular, the other regular, are observable in music, each signalizing its own form of orientation in time.

Irregularly spaced emphases are characteristic of a *prosical* melodic line. [52] The emphasized tones may receive their relative prominence through several circumstances: they may be accorded greater length than their neighbors (i.e., "agogic" accent) ; or greater volume (i.e., "dynamic" accent). Or they may acquire greater influence from placement in exposed positions in the melodic curve (i.e., "inflective" accent) ; they may be reached, for example, by skip, or they may lie at either peak or in the center of a line of upward or downward pitch motion. Furthermore a given tone may carry more than one of these kinds of emphasis at the same time. Differences in degree of emphasis thus secured, which in prosical melody occur unsystematically in the tone line, offer distinguishable points of comparison in the time flow. Their irregular placement is motivated by rhetorical interests, and issues from the larger structural and expressive objectives of the melody; or, the irregular placement of emphases may be the direct result of the inflectional and rhetorical demands of an associated text.

Regularly distributed stresses, on the other hand, are characteristic of a *metrical* melodic line. [70] But equidistant emphases can conceivably be laid off only as they occur along a stream of substantially equidistant pulses, whose regularity of flow serves as a measure of the lapse of time between stresses. Such a series of pulses is measured into equal pulse groups, however, not solely by the regular occurrence of dynamically accented tones in the melody. For the regularity of grouping, once set up, is

8]

given support by a confirmatory periodic fluctuation of the listener's attention, which tends to maintain itself in such a way that regularly recurring moments of greater vividness of attention continue to coincide expectantly with regularly spaced points of greater intensity of tone. There are thus perceivable but two basic pulse groupings, double and triple, and all metrical melody lies over one or the other of these types of meter, or over regular or irregular multiples of them.

In fact, the evolving of higher metrical groups is not only possible but unavoidable, since the moments of greater vividness of attention are themselves not equal in intensity. From the greater and lesser emphases which result, there rises a compound meter, double or triple, and above that supermeasures — more often double though sometimes triple — which together carry the limited propulsion of simple meter over the threshold into the broader pulses of structure. Since it is the metrical impulses of the melodic time pattern itself which launch the periodic fluctuations of attention in the listener's response, the attention adjusts itself in confirmation when this pattern changes, either in the pace of the underlying pulses or in the grouping of them. But this power of adaptation weakens as the expanse of comparison enlarges, and longer spans are measured not by meter but by various structural units and their comparisons.

In metrical, as in prosical melody, there may occur, in addition to dynamic accent, both the agogic emphasis of greater relative length and the inflective emphasis accruing from position; but there is this difference, that while these emphases are, all three alike, the basic articulation of prosical melody, in metrical melody the last two are superadditions to the scheme of dynamic accents indigenous to meter. These added emphases, which may coincide with and hence reinforce the regular metrical accents, or which by irregularity of occurrence may compete with or temporarily submerge the latter (as in "syncopation"), are as in prosical melody rhetorical in origin, and as such are interpretative in value. This interplay of metrical and rhetorical emphases forms a composite *accent pattern,* which is responsible for much of the individuality of the rhythmic pattern of the tone line.

It must finally be pointed out that the various kinds of time comparison described involve relations which maintain their character in different frames of pace; that is, the unit of motion may flow within limits at various rates of speed. It is further true that this rate of flow may be subtly accelerated or decelerated without impairment of the time relations within the frame of pace represented. Such modifications of the basic rate of flow are both justified and necessitated as means of throwing into rhetorical relief particular details of the pitch-time pattern. With this flexing of pace, volume nuance is closely coördinated, the two functioning as qualifying and interpretative forces in the rendering of tone pattern.

Volume comparison, important as it is in the aesthetic realization of tone and time relations, rests on no such tangible a basis as do these latter. For the perceiver possesses no faculty for spontaneously measuring volume change comparable in precision to the sense of pitch, or to the sense of elapsing time through periodic movement. Volume comparison is therefore to a considerable extent the immediate and direct sensation of expanding or contracting mass of sound. [52]

But while volume change lacks a basis for exact and sustained measurement, the relations gain sufficient definition from the fact that fluctuations of volume are felt in successive local frames of intensity. The more extensive comparisons of volume are then perceived between the average volume levels of successive frames. The area of these frames of volume reference is likely to correspond in general to well defined spans of the design. Volume change is the more fluent and responsive in support of the evolving inflections of pattern, and the more useful as a collateral orientation, for its imprecision and consequent plasticity.

The essence of melodic motion is onward. It is natural, therefore, in the more specific orientation of the melodic line, that points of rhythmic emphasis should stand forth as focal points of motion. Each such point extends its influence in both directions, so that there is in its territory a movement of flow toward the instant of emphasis, the instant of arrival itself, and a movement of flow past it. The phenomenon of approach to a point of emphasis is that of anacrusis; the phenomenon of motion carrying past the instant of emphasis is one of "lag". The tones of the melodic line may thus be thought of as crystallizing into pitch-time pattern units around points of emphasis.

The completion of each pattern unit is attended by a sense of breathing or punctuation. The lighter of these punctuation points in the melodic line may be called caesuras; the greater ones are *cadences*, which constitute in themselves controlling points of emphasis, the approach to which is strengthened by subordinate points of emphasis along the route of approach. The concept of the cadence is thus one of increasing imminence in approach to and arrival at the point of consummation of the pattern. [52, 71, 44, 70]

Cadences in the course of the progressing melodic line are themselves also of varying degrees of tonal and rhythmic emphasis. The unit of melodic pattern, the tone relations of which have gained their significance through orientation in pitch, time, and volume, thus receives ultimate orientation in its own cadence among cadences.

Melodic pattern, the components of which we have examined as motion, reaches the listener as audible tone through an instrumental or vocal medium. Every medium has its own characteristics of tone quality which give it individuality and which may make it an appropriate vehicle for various kinds of melody. The melodic line thus comes to the listener clothed in a sensuously evocative TIMBRE, which imparts reality to the pattern. Tone quality is an attribute exterior to the organic tone relations of melody, and scarcely enters into the determination of pattern as such. Its contribution to musical effect is therefore that of a companion to the other sensuous elements in the musical impression.

MELODIC IDENTITY

The melodic line, as patterned tone motion rendered in an enhancing tone quality, must now finally be accepted as more than a mere animated mechanism. Its manifestation of an impulse so productive that a self-renewing motion is generated; its endowment with a purposefulness so definite that the illusion of advance is created; its possession of a diversity of motion so rich that constantly fresh constellations of detail unfold; its revelation of an integrative force so convincing that a quality of reasoned organization is felt; its embodiment of a genius so potent that a unique response of thought and mood is awakened and sustained in the listener: — these characteristics give to melody what Combarieu has termed "sense". That is, melodic motion, through the distinctiveness of its combined pattern of pitch, time, and volume relations, and through its "expressive" potential, displays personality, identity. In short, melody is *idea,* — not idea in the sense of accredited symbolical meaning for given patterns, but *musical* idea, complete and intelligible in its own right, needing no further meaning, and incapable of it except through added (often gratuitously added) association. From a genesis in ideas in this sense, and through a continuing projection of them, the musical organism as a whole evolves.

The stuff of music is then *melody as idea.* In fact, though its three-dimensional motion forms but a single tone line, melody constitutes a self-sufficient and mature vehicle of musical communication — the idiom of MONODY.

II. TEXTURE

PATTERNED MOTION IN A COMPOSITE OF LINES

Although music of high artistic import exists in the monodic idiom with its single line of motion, the greater part of the literature of music finds expression in idioms involving more than one tone line at a time. The union of several lines of motion produces a composite motion, which is the product of relations of tones in *both* successive and simultaneous motion. This significant concept in music is TEXTURE. The coalescing of the three-dimensional motion of each line with that of every other line generates an encompassing textural motion, through the interplay of the factors of which music gains much of its forward impulse, its organic cohesion, and its light and shade.

The defining characteristic of this motion is its comprisal of lines displaying relatively different kinds and degrees of value as ideas. Not only are the simultaneous tone lines likely to exhibit differences, but the differences will frequently take the form of disparities. The pitch line may accordingly range from an almost straight contour to one of complicated curve. At the same time, the pattern may vary from comparative inaction to intense activity. The combination of the two patterns may result in an elementary or a self-effacing tone line, or in the highest melodic individuality.

On such differences in value among the lines rests the distinctive phenomenon of *textural perspective,* in which one line or another appears to stand in the auditory foreground, others in the nearer or farther background. [33, 74] While these differences among the lines are intrinsic to the ideas themselves by virtue of their pitch and time patterns, textural perspective is given auditory reinforcement by subtly adjusted counterbalances among the volume curves of the lines, each volume pattern conforming to the interests and intent of its own tone line. The result is in effect a stereoscopic revelation of textural relations.

Though the tone lines which enter into a given texture may assert certain contrasted values, they do not necessarily continue to maintain their initial qualities and relative importance. Interchange of values may occur as one idea relinquishes its place of prominence to another: different lines at different times may occupy the foreground or background. Textural light and shade, as well as fruitful organic rearrangements, result from such shifting of the focus of interest from line to line. [46a] At the same time the lines may close in or spread apart in a variety of spacings, in the interests of diversification of the textural balance.

Nor need there be a constantly maintained number of simultaneous lines in the texture. Essential addition and subtraction of lines may take place; or lines may disintegrate and disappear and new ones be grafted transiently into the composite motion. A thinning or thickening of the texture results, which may be accomplished gradually or suddenly. [2, 1] There may even occur massed rearrangements of tone which temporarily obliterate the linear constitution of the texture. But always there remains intact, except perhaps momentarily, a defining thread of melodic sustainment. The elaborate variety of composite motion which arises in these activities of texture is inexhaustible and supplies the leaven of textural vitality.

While textural motion is forward in direction, it involves at the same time simultaneous relationships among the coinciding tones of the lines. Both the conspicuousness and the significance of these relations of coincidence will vary according to the textural distribution of values among the tone lines. At the one extreme these relations may be a mere passive by-product of the interaction of several lines of marked melodic value. [26, 10] On the other hand, the relations among tones sounding at the same moment may be so specific that tone blocks, or *chords,* are asserted or clearly implied in the textural motion. [29, 53, 60, 49]

The existence of these tone blocks and their perceivability as such depend on strong systematic relations among the tones, as distinguished from transient and casual coincidences of textural motion. The systematic nature of the relations may arise from acoustical influence and precedents, or as in certain recent systems they may follow unacoustical, and hence in a sense arbitrary formulae of the composer or school.

[15

Tone combinations based on such systematic relations among the members exhibit a notable individuality, on the basis of which two general types of combination are discernible, *consonance* and *dissonance*. The consonant chord, both as a tone mass and in terms of motion, is marked by the sensation of comparative repose, of freedom from tension. Its tones tend to fuse into a homogeneous whole, felt as substantially unified within itself. The physical criterion of this unity is a relatively simple acoustical relation among the tones.

The dissonant chord displays traits which are in general the reverse of those of the consonant. The sensation is now one of pressure, of relative tension. The tones are individualized in a resistance to fusion, with the result that they hold apart from one another in suspense, forming an identifiable but temporary whole, which is always on the brink of "resolution". The dissonant chord is physically the product of an acoustically more complex relation of tones.

In spite of these well defined differences between consonance and dissonance, the latter are not absolutes. This is true because the ultimate *musical* difference between them is aesthetic, that is, is based upon their effects on the listener. But the listener's impression of repose *versus* tension is itself variable according to the conditioning influence of familiarity and to the particular stylistic context of a given consonant or dissonant situation. [25, 42, 51, 45, 5, 14, 76, 74, 68, 24, 58, 10, 69]

In aesthetic terms, the value of tension and release lies in their enhancement of one another. Tensions may be built up in succession to pyramidal intensity, but must ultimately find common release in the function of relative consonance. [14] The prevailing direction of the motion created by the juxtaposition of dissonance and consonance is movement from the former to the latter. A dissonance tends to resolve not only to consonance in general but to particular consonances. It is from such a complementary relation of the consonant and dissonant functions that a substantial part of the drive of musical motion is derived.

Two consonant chords (major and minor) and a wide variety of dissonant chords are conventionally distinguishable. Each chord possesses an identity or flavor of its own which may be thought of as *chord color*. [29, 59, 24]

Distinctive as chord colors are in themselves, their destiny however is motion. From this standpoint chord movements reveal both a passive aspect of succession and an active one of progression. As one chord succeeds another, a transient color sensation of the movement itself is felt, — the waning impression of the first chord carried over as a fringe into the second. The more positive aspect of chord motion suggests, on the other hand, the effect of chord proceeding to chord with intent, often of chord driving toward chord. In such chord motion the pressure of progression is strongly supported by correlated rhythmic action.

Chord motion, however, can scarcely exist as an independent, self-justifying activity, certainly not for more than a moment at a time. It is inextricably bound up with melodic motion, which both preinfluences and coexists with the chord motion.

While the interaction of melody and chords is a unanimous one, there may nevertheless arise temporary conflicts between the forward pitch and rhythmic movements of melody and the block formations of chords. Tones essential to the character of the melodic line may, for the moment, crowd out expected tones of the chord. Melodic dissonance against the chord results and is resolved as

[17

the course of the melody finally permits the normal but momentarily displaced chord tone to arrive. Such melodic conflicts against the chord as this may occur in more than one tone line at once. [5, 65, 74]

The simultaneous and forward tone movements of texture, as they consolidate—or by implication partially consolidate — into chord progressions motivated by melody, may now be recognized as the phenomenon of HARMONY. The time organization of these successive movements forms a harmonic rhythm and the relations among the chord progressions in their forward motion compose a *harmonic pattern*. As in the contour of melody the organically more significant tones produce among themselves a supercontour, so chords more than one remove apart in the harmonic pattern may also join in a progression of higher relations.

MELODICO-HARMONIC ORIENTATION

Patterned harmonic motion, as with melodic motion, can be perceived in the nature of the case only in terms of comparison of known factors. These individual factors of harmonic relation are chords, or implied chords, systematically formed from the tones of the various modes. The chords of a given mode owe their relation to one another to their mutual relation to the chord of reference of that mode. The chord of reference, containing as its chief element the tone of reference, acquires priority through its use as a point of harmonic arrival. The chord relations of the mode thus constitute a system of harmonic orientation, completely coördinate with the tone relations of melody in that mode. Such mode families of chords supply the harmonic vocabulary of a great proportion of musical works.

Harmonic movement with respect to the chord of reference may proceed with various degrees of definition. In less emphatic kinds of harmonic motion, the chords succeed one another without marked definiteness of directional indication. [38] In the more active interrelation of the chords of a mode to the chord of reference, each chord performs a distinct function in the course of the motion toward the chord of reference. The chord family thus becomes a hierarchy of chords, and the chord of reference is invested with a positive superiority which constitutes it a *tonic* chord. The gravitational drive toward that chord, with varying but purposeful degrees of urgency by way of other chords of the mode, is HARMONIC TONALITY. [32, 48] One chord in particular of the other chords of the mode offers the most forceful approach to the tonic; that chord, called the dominant, is empowered to exert its special function largely because of its significant acoustical relation to the tonic.

The same forces which implement melodic tonality enter into harmonic tonality; that is, the tonic derives its quality as a focus of harmonic motion partly from acoustical sources, partly through its relatively frequent occurrence and conspicuous placement, and partly through a psychological anticipation of its predictable arrival. Strong rhythmic confirmation of the chord progressions is also an important factor in definiteness of harmonic tonality.

In harmony, again as in the case of melody, the vocabulary need not be confined exclusively to the tones of the mode. Chords may be formed which include one chromatic tone or several. The chromatic chords thus produced derive their orientation from chords within the mode, and their progressions therefore take place under a widened influence of the tonic. [59, 76]

It may now be seen that the tone relations of mode,

expressible within certain limits in melodic motion, are given an amplified exploitation through the addition of harmonic motion, and that tonality of melody and the tonal gravitation of harmony are actually collateral aspects of a single larger tonal phenomenon. Textural orientation is thus completed in the mutual activities of melody and harmony, and harmony joins with melody as a significant part of the substance of the musical idea.

Harmonic formations and relations may also be conceived in other than modal and tonal terms. In atonal styles the systematic relation of the tones of a chord may be based on unacoustical, independent formulae, in consequence of which dissonance becomes the norm. In the absence of a tonic as such, chord motion is strongly influenced by melody or combined melodies, by the inducements of color successions, and by the purposeful interplay of different degrees of dissonance. [10, 58]

IDIOM

We have seen, in the multilinear relations of texture, that diversity in individuality among the tone lines is common. As a result, according to the particular adjustment of values, various types of texture are distinguishable, so characteristic in their composition that basic idioms are formed. In addition to monody, the textureless idiom of melody alone, the two chief such idioms are POLYPHONY and HOMOPHONY (or monophony).

The idiom of polyphony is marked by a prevailing equivalence — not necessarily equality — among the tone lines. The lines are matched against one another and the texture is one of diffused or distributed melodic interest. [25, 26, 51, 4, 32, 74, 35] In the textural interweaving of the melodies harmonic relations are frequently revealed. These may be of such a kind that the harmony appears to be an unassertive or even negative coincidence of the melodic relations; [38, 30, 62] or, at the opposite, the harmonic scheme may be so specific as to influence the actual nature and course and relation of the melodies themselves. [7, 32]

In the atonal system, the melodies may run counter to one another in a dissonant independence which fundamentally precludes systematic chordal implications. [10] In the polytonal system, two or more lines, each in its own tonality, may be combined at their own pitch localities in a polyphony of lines. While it is conceivable that each line may be heard in its own tonal orientation, there is nevertheless a textural union of their identities as lines, which results in varying degrees of textural dissonance according to the number of and the disparities among the tonalities engaged. [36] Whatever the ingredients may be, the essential quality of polyphony, that is, competitive interest among lines, remains.

The idiom of homophony, on the other hand, is characterized by a prevailing disparity of values among the lines of the texture. They are unmatched in individuality and there is a concentration of melodic interest in one line at a time. [45, 56, 55, 60] In the emphatic auditory foreground lies this chief line, "the melody", with other lines of less or little special identity and indeterminate in number and consistency, forming or implying chords. This attending harmonic motion, "the harmonic accompaniment", supports and confirms the primary line of melody. But however variable in linear terms the textural incorporation of these chords is, there is certain to be present, except for brief intermittency, an underlying line, which collaborates with the melody, and which has its own particular kind of identity, that is, "the bass". Homophony is thus a texture governed by the interassociation of a chief melody (usually the topmost line of the texture, although not necessarily so) and a bass tone line (invariably the lowest). Each of these lines contributes its particular function to the constitution of the idiom.

Less sharply defined functional relations among the lines of the texture than those exhibited in polyphony and homophony produce other idioms, hybrid in character and drawing for the elements of their textural organism on resources borrowed from the two fundamental idioms. These hybrid idioms, of many varieties, have no benefit of name, and are designated loosely by such terms as "semi-polyphony", [8a] "homophony with polyphonic detail", [46a] and so forth.

MEDIUM

In the actual formulation of texture, the exigencies of the particular instrumental or vocal medium for which the texture is conceived exert a modifying influence. This may be a limitation, which confines the textural application to the more favorable capacities of a given medium. The invention of a polyphonic texture for the violin, for example, presents forbidding restrictions. The more significant influence, however, is that which at the outset shapes the ideas themselves so as actually to exploit a texture idiomatic to the medium in hand.

In the textural combining of lines, the tone qualities of more than one medium or the differences in quality within the range of a single medium may be brought together. Different qualities may be adroitly intermingled and contrasted, and innumerable fresh blends evoked by combination. Coördination of the tone qualities with different kinds of textural spacement, or high or low pitch placement, may evoke impressions figuratively termed light or dark, warm or cool. The combination of tone qualities may remain stable for the time being, [33a] or it may incessantly fluctuate. [16, 76, 67] The scheme which underlies such interplays of tone quality is a *timbre pattern*.

But the pattern of tone qualities enjoys no tangible existence of its own, occupies no dimension of the motion: it is completely accessory to the tone pattern. In this capacity it gives sensuous intensity to the other patterns with which it is enmeshed. A given timbre may even seem so appropriate to a particular musical idea or type of idea, that the idea is personified in that quality. Of greater importance still, the timbre pattern underscores and throws into relief value distinctions among the ideas of the texture, frequently with the added coöperation of volume distinctions, and hence contributes substantially to a discriminative realization of the design. [9, 46a, 76, 23]

*　　*

*

It is evident that texture, as an amalgamation of melodic and harmonic pattern, generates various associated patterns, which are actually only particular aspects of the whole. There is thus an over-all textural rhythm, which is the comprehensive rhythm of all of the time relations comprising the motion. There is an over-all textural nuance, consisting of incessant and elaborate adjustments in the volumes of tone against tone and line against line, which unfolds its own course of development cognately to the organism of ideas itself. There is an over-all textural color of consonance and dissonance, which exhibits as the melodic and harmonic ideas proceed an evolving flux of tensions and releases. Finally, there is an over-all textural timbre, which gives aural definition and sensuous distinctiveness to the other patterns. That is to say, in the fusion of the several patterns there exists an inclusive *textural pattern* which is the very essence of the organic motion of music, the web of the ideas themselves.

III. DESIGN

We have so far dealt with ideas as mere constituents, capable of acquiring significance only as they are given reason for being in a corporate whole. This whole is an organism or DESIGN, initiated in a local *formulation* of ideas, and evolved through their *projection* into the larger pattern of the whole, in faithful realization of an "expressive" intent.

THE FORMULATION OF IDEAS: LOCAL DESIGN

The materials for the formulation of local design consist in brief pattern units or kernels of idea called *motives*. [8a, 14, 76] These are in turn embedded in ideas of long enough span and of significant enough value to assert themselves as the basic subject matter of a musical work or important part of a work. These more amply formulated ideas are *themes*, [60, 74] and their quality as initially defined dominates the whole work, even though they may incur profound modification in the course of projection of the design.

The organic differences between polyphony on the one hand, and monody and homophony on the other, signify in the nature of the case such inherent differences of principle in the formulation of ideas, that these two idiomatically dissimilar types of design must be considered separately.

In polyphony the characteristic methods of formulating

24]

ideas arise from the nature of the idiom itself as plural linear motion. There are two chief typical forms of presentation, both of them embodying the principle of concurrent statement in two or more lines: one is the establishment of polyphonic relations between a melody and itself, the other of relations between two or among several different melodies.

The former method consists in the statement of a melody in one line of the texture, succeeded by an early restatement of it, in identical form or with limited modifications, in another line or in several different lines in succession. Each line, when it has finished with the theme, continues with relevant material. The idea may follow itself directly, [4] or it may overlap itself; [37] in the latter case, each ensuing presentation begins before the previous one has finished and a relation of "canon" among the lines is set up. This typically polyphonic method of formulation is appropriately called IMITATION and is the characteristic way in which the structural principle of repetition manifests itself locally in polyphony. The simultaneous lines are given an inseparable organic connection by the distribution among them of one idea, which each line possesses in turn.

The other typical method of formulation in polyphony is the simultaneous statement of two or more melodies in such a relation that one of them constitutes the basic idea of the structure and the others play the rôle of counterfoil and companion to the central idea. The essential or fixed melody is called the *cantus firmus* and the companions are *counterpoints* to it and to one another. The associated melodies may form a contrapuntal texture with their cantus firmus in positions above, below, or around it. [43, 9] The relation of counterpoint to cantus firmus is one of at least partial contrast.

[25

In the formulation of polyphonic texture the separate lines are likely to maintain a sufficient degree of independence so that their spans differ in length and their cadences accordingly fall at different points. [51, 74] This staggered distribution of cadences throughout the texture gives to polyphony its remarkable degree of continuity of local organization.

In monody and homophony the idiomatic method of formulation is the presentation of ideas, or fractions of them, in successive statement in one line. In this type of formulation it is the nature of the melodic organism to evolve the enlarging pattern through the agency of a series of temporarily incomplete but related patterns, the interdependent incompletenesses of which lead forward in sustained expectation to fulfilment in the completed design.

In one type of relation, the ideas may follow one another with homogeneous diversity of content, with planned differences of cadential arrival among the several spans, and in irregular lengths. From such patterning a rhapsodic or "through-composed" design is formed. [29, 31]

A different and peculiarly cogent way of relating successive ideas, in integrative movement toward completion, is that of pairing. In this association the relation of the members of a pair is one of complementary interdependence, a relation resting on the function of proposition or *thesis* in the first idea of the pair, so formulated as to demand response or *antithesis* in the second idea. [47] This functional behavior of the two ideas springs from an exploitation of compensated similarities and diversities within the common ground of the pair. The instrumentalities for this distinction between the spans are the patterns of the ideas themselves, the nature of the terminal cadences, and the relative lengths of the spans. Thus, while the ideas must be homogeneous enough to belong together, in fact, are likely to contain conspicuous common materials, they also display suggestive differences at strategic points. In consequence, influential comparisons are invited, such as between the initial motives, or between the final motives, or between mid-peaks of their motion. In particular, their ends are likely to be thrown into relief against one another. At such points as these the pitch contours of the ideas, or their rhythmic patterns, or both, differ but are specifically interlocked in meaning. The cadences at the ends of the two ideas are contrasted in such a way that the first claims less emphasis or weight than the second, is comparatively incomplete and expectant in character, and seeks compensation in the greater degree of finality of the second cadence. This relation is typical when the former cadence is a dominant and the latter a tonic.

In further support of the complementary relation between the members of the pair, the two spans, in formal designing, are likely to be of equal length. But the affinity of the two members is not dependent on such precision, and various compensations may arise to offset inequality of length in the interests of more flexible forms of collaboration. In fact, a number of ideas in series, of variable lengths, and with cadences which defer completion, may in conjunction produce a chain of units, each one of which is a partial thesis to its successor, and at the same time a partial antithesis to its predecessor. [75] Pairing under such conditions is implied rather than specifically realized.

It is now evident that the controlled incompleteness of the thesis creates an expectation which is satisfied fully or partially by the antithesis: the two ideas are counterbalanced against one another. This complementary relation between successive members of a pair of ideas is the phenomenon of PERIODICITY. The incomplete member spans are *phrases* and the whole is a sentence or *period*. This principle of formulation, with whatever degrees of subtlety or whatever incidental irregularities it may manifest itself, is basic to the monodic and homophonic organisms.

The periodic correlation of the members of a pair is not a mere static formula, for in their organic relation there inheres a function of alternation, which imparts a rhythmic impulse to the larger pattern, as the term "periodic" itself suggests. This is *structural rhythm;* [15] it signifies the fusion of the melodic, harmonic, and textural rhythms, which are its components, into an evolving composite rhythm of design.

STRUCTURAL ORIENTATION

We have seen that the action of melody and harmony is purposeful and that their motion is directional in character, due to specific forms of orientation which they bring to the design in which they are participants. Thus in melody there is a tone of reference, chief of the tones of the mode family, and in harmony a chord of reference; these act as focal points respectively and jointly of tone and chord movements, and, as such, form structural arrival points of the melodic and harmonic spans. We must now note further that within the jurisdiction of these chief points of reference lesser subpoints may exist, which serve as local arrivals along the route of motion toward a chief point of arrival at the end of the larger span. These subpoints within the mode are, in comparison with the chief point, temporary, unstable, but anticipatory, — predictive of an ultimate stable arrival at the final point, that is, the tonic.

In a similar way, on a larger scale, the chief tones and chords of reference may reveal among themselves a relation to one of their number, which exercises the power of a superpoint of reference or tonality of reference, and thus becomes the head of a hierarchy of tonalities and the ultimate structural point of reference of an entire musical work. Each tonality, with reference to the others, is then felt to occupy a particular pitch locality or *key*. In the articulation of the design the process of disestablishing the jurisdiction of one tonality and of establishing that of another is called *modulation*. [39, 56, 76] These relations of locality constitute among themselves a system of STRUCTURAL TONALITY. [48] They may exist among modes of the same kind or of any number of different kinds, since this is an orientation of modes with respect to their localities, not to their kinds as modes.

In the orientation of design through the constructive operation of these relations, a fundamental law of economy — that the relations be centripetal, that the movement be circular in character — asserts itself. The involutions of design based on this principle entail therefore the establishment of a central tonality, digression from it to others, and the ultimate reëstablishment of the original tonality. [45, 18] In designs of considerable extent there will be formed, within the whole, areas under the control of subtonalities, each area with its own inner scheme of relation among the component tonalities. Such an interior scheme may be a circular one of digression and return to the subtonality, [46b] or it may be a cursive one of changing tonalities, [7] according to the interests of the design as a whole. The larger the design the more far-flung must be the scheme of tonalities, in order to provide the necessary variety of location for a multiplicity of ideas and structural divisions. [14]

The exact process of orientation, in styles based on different structural and aesthetic premises, will vary in character and specificness. Furthermore, within the general frame of any type of orientation, there may occur subordinate deviations from the norm. The orienting operations may be momentarily suppressed, or interrupted, with consequent deferment of their effect; or the course marked out may be subjected to artistically contrived conflicts, such that the implied orientation remains unfulfilled. These controlled irregularities offer powerful resources in the design, through the varying degrees of pressure which they afford within the structural motion.

In atonal music special forms of orientation have been devised, which give action and intelligibility to the structural motion. In order to claim soundness, they must of course retain the functions of local preparation for landing and of landing (though not that of specific "aiming"), as well as the function of differentiable degrees of weight of landing, so that structural comparisons may be possible. [58, 10] The larger design is sometimes given conviction through systematically recurrent master-patterns or "tone-rows", which retain their stabilizing value even when subjected to subtle transformations. In any case, whatever the epoch or formula of the music may be, some sort of orientation must exist as the index of rationality in design.

It is now evident that an important *modus operandi* of orientation in design is cadence comparison. Cadences are the signposts of direction in design, and only through organization and contrast is the varied array of relations of span within span given implementation. We may conceive of a hierarchy of cadences, then, embedded in the design of a musical work and offering degrees of finality of arrival, that is, of cadential weight, as the indispensable basis of logically oriented structural motion. As a part of and in support of the larger pattern there is therefore in every design a *cadence pattern,* the contours of which form one aspect of the framework of the design as a whole.

No hard and fast line exists between the operations of the local and of the extensive design. The methods of local formulation of ideas carry over into the larger process of projection and continue to propagate within it. The extensive design, as it evolves its greater span, contains the local, is supported by it, even partially shaped by it.

The process of projection follows two basic principles. The first — that of addition of spans to one another in various forms of relation, until the logical extent of design has been achieved — is the corner-stone of extensification. The second principle, that of internal expansion, involves the sustainment of the inherent reach of the span by reproductive inner growth. The reciprocal application of these two resources produces full foundation for the most extensive and elaborate designs. The longer the extent the more complicated will be the interaction of these processes.

The Interrelation of Spans

In the placement of spans end to end both disjunct and conjunct forms of contact are found, symptomatic of contrary attributes of design. When the contact of spans is prevailingly disjunct a sectional type of design is generated, in which the emphasis lies upon a marked antithesis of ideas and the constructive effects which can be drawn from such contrast. [56, 34, 60] In general, the sectional principle tends to characterize the more elementary designs or those of highly formal complexion.

A conjunct contact of the spans of a design suggests, on the other hand, a continuous and flexible type of organization. The ends of spans may overlap (in polyphony they actually dovetail) , the sense of divisioning is minimized, and a sustainment of motion results which is favorable to protracted design and to an unremitting evolving of idea, in contrast to an antithetical opposition of ideas. [3, 74, 17, 76, 67] A salient agent involved in the maintenance of such continuity is fluctuating tonality, which makes a majority of the arrival points incomplete and anticipatory. In spite of their differences, both forms of organization hold a significant energy of motion favorable for projection of the design.

In the succession of spans to form the larger design, certain fundamental aesthetic principles dominate the process of projection. They are the principles, common to all of the arts, of *similarity, diversity,* and *proportion.* In their mutual application, the terms in which they operate are those of material (motive, theme, division) and of locality (modal, tonal or other) . Through the interdependent behavior of these factors the principles of similarity, diversity, and proportion permeate the fabric of design, manifesting themselves in ways unique to music.

The introduction of elements of similarity in the course of a musical design is a response to a deep-lying sense of economy. In an art in which the pattern is in constant motion, and in which earlier spans have disappeared beyond recovery, except through renewal in the memory, such backward reference is the more imperative. The projection of the design on the basis of similarity is achieved through various forms of *repetition.* The materials subjected to repetition may be such smaller units as the motive or the phrase, or even a minute extracted detail of pitch or time pattern; or whole divisions may be reintroduced and relocated in the larger design.

Repetition of idea may be immediate or it may occur after digression. In the former case it supplies chiefly a touch of local emphasis and may have the effect of momentarily suspending the larger progress of the design, without materially influencing its general proportions or logic. [63] Following digression, repetition becomes one of the chief forces in determining the arrangements and extent, and hence the nature, of the design. [22, 47, 48, 64]

Repetition of idea may furthermore be exact or it may entertain essential modifications, but not great enough ones to obliterate the unifying effect of reuse. Exact repetition is formal in significance and carries with it certain static limitations of the design. [46b] Repetition involving modification, on the other hand, is the very foundation of controlled evolution in design, and constitutes a basic tool in shaping the higher types of structure. [48a, 14a]

The device of repetition is also significantly applied in terms of pitch locality. This is in effect a *re*orientation. Return to an earlier locality, either temporarily, or in a circular closing of the design, offers an economy of perception which is indispensable in its clarification of the organism and in the sense of satisfaction which it imparts. [48, 64, 18]

Important, however, as repetitions of idea and locality are individually, it is in their coördination that they reach their highest structural value. For repetition of idea is immeasurably strengthened when it coincides with reorientation in the original locality; and return of locality powerfully invites return of idea. In fact, repetition of idea in a changed location, energetic as its implications are, contains within itself a demand for an eventual simultaneous return of both idea and locality. The introduction of similarities of any sort is ultimately centripetal in its effect on design.

A peculiar form of immediate repetition, involving exact or slightly modified pitch-time pattern, but coupled with shift in pitch locality, is found in the device of *sequence*. It consists of several repetitions of a motive or phrase pattern at successive systematically raised or lowered pitch localities. The effect is one of a mounting or descending logic of motion, which exerts a strong forward momentum of expectation in the design. The device is a mechanistic one if applied literally or if continued through too many repetitions of the original pattern unit; it gains considerable flexibility and sophistication if slight modifications of the pattern are introduced in some of the repetitions. A sequence may unfold within the scope of a single mode or tonality, [47] or its links may advance through modulation. [56] The sequential process may involve the pattern of melody alone, more often those of melody and harmony in coöperation; it carries its systematic effect into the actual organization of the design itself. [74] It may enter both the simultaneous relations of polyphonic texture [4] and the successive ones of homophony. [56]

It is not to be supposed that literal or even approximate backward references of idea and locality are the sole support of the economy of similarities in design. Less palpable but equally competent is the maintenance of a progressive *relevancy* of idea, under the influence of which the design advances through the steady incorporation of comparatively small increments of new material. The composition of the material is in an incessant gradual change from old to new, seeming to feed upon itself as the design evolves. [73, 17a]

But similarity functions only when afforded the compensation of diversity, the agent of which in the projection of design is *contrast*. Like repetition it operates in the fields of both material and locality, and seeks its most potent manifestations in a coördination of the two factors.

Contrast occurs, with varying types of effect and contribution to the design, at different levels of complication. In its simplest terms it brings forward a new idea, in which case the process of projection, in the actual furtherance of the design, reverts temporarily to formulation. The statement of a new idea for contrast is greatly enhanced by its placement in a contrasted locality. This combination represents contrast at a maximum; it is direct and vigorous in the promotion of the design. [66, 17]

It is nevertheless obvious that the degree of contrast must fall within convincing aesthetic boundaries and that the appropriate amount and quality of newness are contingent upon the context into which they are drawn. Suddenly introduced contrasts, either of idea or locality, or both, in the interests of rhetorical or dramatic effect, are assimilable and valuable, however, if they are compatible with the larger relevancy of ideas which encompasses every rational design.

More discriminating manifestations of the value of contrast than the introduction of a new idea involve retention of some kind of appreciable contact with previous ideas. This contact may take different forms, with consequent differences of effect upon the design.

The most limited of such applications of contrast is the actual retention of the old idea, and the repetition of it with a *change of context*. It is thus new surroundings, rather than a new fundamental idea, which supplies the element of contrast. A familiar instance is the device of the "ground bass", [54] in which a phrase repeats itself a number of times in the bass, attended by a changing melodic and harmonic superstructure. In polyphony the repetition of a melody with a new counterpoint is a further case in illustration. [3]

Less literal in retention of the old idea is the devising of a *variant* of it, or a series of variants. This process operates through the consistent alteration of conspicuous factors of the original idea, while yet enough of its character is retained to identify the source of the new version. [48a] Contrast within the framework of the old idea is thus produced, and at the same time substantial advance is secured through the introduction of fresh features. The "theme with variations" is an example of a sustained application of this device. [33a] In polyphony the "inversion", "augmentation", "diminution", or "retrogression" of a theme represent special manifestations of the variant.

But these procedures are somewhat static in the generation of contrast. A more marked contrast, which is indebted to the old idea, but at the same time enjoys virtual independence, is secured through *derivation*. The derived idea is synthesized from elements detached from a former idea or from more than one, but in such terms that the new idea achieves a separate identity of its own. [40, 17, 17a]

Of all the processes of procuring contrast, which yet retain a degree of anchorage in past ideas, that of *development* is the most potent in its contribution to the organic quality of the design. In contradistinction to derivation, which contrives a formed new idea from the old, development is the generation of a constant stream of ideas of new implication, not only from earlier sources, but successively from one another. Fluently changing locality is an indispensable support of the proceeding. Development is the actual evolution of idea in process, bringing forth its own substance as it advances. It is the living fruit of a creative adjustment between old and new, a reconciliation of two opposing forces of design, in the union of which a greater force is brought into being. Development is the essence of "similarity with contrast" and as such the highest manifestation of the aesthetic of design. [2, 14, 76, 17, 68]

The application of the principle of proportion in the projection of musical ideas involves the adjustment against one another of the extents of the structure (and, in a special sense, of the climaxes*) , so that there is no finally unbalanced conflict of interests among them.

But it must be noted that in music length as such, except comparatively brief length, is subject to only the most general measurements by the listener. In fact, the greater the length, the less exact becomes his sense of elapsed time. It is true that the constitution of a longer span from easily identified and measurable shorter units facilitates a conception of the length of the whole. But a built-up total of lengths loses precision for the listener as it enlarges. This imprecision, however, is of relatively little consequence in the listener's perception of proportions, since an important and less literal factor than mere physical length enters into the concept of extent. This is the factor of weight, that is, the loading of a given length with a superior concentration of idea. Extent, as distinguished from physical length, is hence measured by the listener in the relative terms of approximate length qualified by weight. It is in this aesthetic sense that extents play against one another in establishing the proportions of design.

In the proportional distribution of extents, their scope is determined by the thematic content. A single idea may stand forth as a unit of extent; or several ideas may group together to form one thematic area, by virtue of the homogeneity of their material or of the bond of a single tonal locality for the entire thematic group. [14] An extent, in proportional terms, measured in length and weight, and

---

* See *The Design Contour*, p. 46 ff.

defined by homogeneity and tonal cohesion, is thus the relative structural space allowed for the activities of a given idea or homogeneous group of ideas. In a broader and less precise sense, it is evident that extents are the relative areas assigned to the operation of similarities and diversities. Proportion is, then, the allocation of extents to ideas according to the requirements of their respective functions in a given design.*

In realization of proportional relations both *symmetrical* and *asymmetrical* organisms may result, as well as those displaying in different parts of their course both of these types of relation.

The simplest manifestation of symmetrical proportion is found in the balanced spans of periodic structure, where either equality of length or equivalence of weight, supported by tonal antithesis and reconciliation, produces an equitable adjustment between the members of the pair. This paired relation may be made the vehicle of enlarged periodic designs rendered in pairs of pairs, and so on to the point of sterility or of the perceiver's inability to co-ordinate the pairing at greater range. Proportions characterized by symmetry of this kind are duple in essence. [47] Symmetrical proportion, but of a different order, may be equally an attribute of designs based on three equivalent divisions. Such triple proportions demonstrate their symmetry through a balance, in idea and tonality, between the force of diversion in the contrasting middle span, and the force of stabilization in the combined first and third spans, alike or similar as they are in idea and locality. [64] These duple and triple adjustments of extent, or their multiples or combinations, susceptible of application in various ways both locally and extensively, represent the

---

* See *The Thematic Functions,* p. 40 ff.

basic procedure in applying symmetrical proportion.

Asymmetrical proportion is merely a controlled deviation from symmetry: the former concept contains the latter. The deviations of asymmetry are aesthetically provocative and their presence serves to impart finesse to the design through the challenge of reconciliation between the regular and the irregular. The disbalance of asymmetry in search of balance is a powerful impulse in design. Deviations from the symmetrical norm may take the form of interpolation of spans into the duple or triple distributions of proportions; [56] or spans may be added in extension of regular lengths, in such a way as to increase both their length and weight. [47] The sense of irregularity arises from the fact that these additions are construed not as extraneous, but as organic parts of the total. More complicated and artful forms of asymmetry are the result of building up intrinsically irregular lengths and weights of extent, the disparities of which are a relief from the obviousness of geometrical regularity.

No more subtle illustration of asymmetry can be found than in the first division of the "sonata-form". This division consists of two contrasted areas coupled by a transition, and distinguished from one another as the area of the first theme and that of a group of second themes in a secondary tonal locality. The first theme is likely to be briefer in length than the group of second themes. But this disparity of length is presumably compensated for by the greater weight of the first theme, and by its strategic location in the main tonality, as compared with the subordinate tonality of the second theme area. The first theme, however, usually stands in some sense incomplete and in suspense at its close, while the second theme area is likely to end with an emphatically conclusive cadence in the secondary tonality. In the aggregate, then, there is a cunningly contrived disproportion between the extents of the first and second themes in favor of the latter. This slight but intentional undercutting of the position of the first theme imparts a propelling quality of expectation to the design, in anticipation of an inevitable later adjustment of the disbalance. [48]

The more subtle or complicated or wide-spread the design is, the more dependent is it upon the interplay of symmetries and asymmetries in the forming of a convincing *pattern of proportions*. But as the extent increases, and there is a diminution in the perceiver's power to measure the lengths and weights entering into the design, a point is finally reached where the grasp of proportions must depend upon the coördination of the climax points of the design.* By their differentiation, spacement, balance, and cumulative relation, these signalize in a still broader sense the final proportional distributions of the design.

The Thematic Functions

The implementing force, which correlates the resources of similarity, diversity, and proportion in the formation of a specific extensive design, springs from the endowment of the ideas with inner qualities of behavior, so that an idea performs a particular function in the context in which it is placed in the design. A given design is, then, in effect, a *function pattern* of ideas, wrought into the very essence of the formulation and projection of those ideas.

The three primary thematic functions, which may be applied in many different ways with correspondingly different resultant designs, are: the function of *statement,* (formulative, as in the presentation of any idea upon its first appearance in the design); the function of *develop-*

---

* See *The Design Contour,* p. 46 ff.

ment, (projective, as in the continuation or diversified exploitation of an idea) ; the function of *restatement,* (reformulative, as in the return to an idea after intervening contrast). In addition to these primary functions, there are three accessory functions, the interjection of which in various ways enriches, fuses, or broadens the design. These are: the function of *introduction,* (predictive, as in the approach to essential ideas through subordinate, anticipatory ones) ; the function of *transition,* (connective, as in the joining of essential ideas through subordinate linkage) ; the function of *conclusion,* (terminative, as in the confirmation of finality through the addition of an extension or a "coda"). [34a, 48, 14, 17]

It is important to realize that a certain function is not permanently attached to a stated idea, or to a single stated position in a design, but that any idea, new or old, may in the course of the design be given the turn which discloses any of these kinds of behavior. The initial function of an idea is thus subject to alterations, according to the new services which that idea is to perform in the course of the design. Fresh functional contexts are created for old ideas. The larger design is hence an interplay of ideas in the act of continually changing their functions. [14, 74]

Nor are these thematic functions mutually exclusive and pure in their quality over a given extent. More often than not they are found in an interlocking activity, one function operating over an inner span within another fuction of greater extent. [14, 27] The developmental and restating functions, for example, are frequently found within a larger span of statement; the transitional function, limited in range by nature, may appear in the midst of any of the other functions; the concluding function may occur with varying degrees of insistence in the course of statement or restatement, or it may appear even within itself.

Design Types and their Conventionalization into "Forms"

The process of design is evidently a nicely proportioned and constantly reproportioned poise between similarity and diversity. In terms of actual ideas, interacting in explicit thematic functions, the effective application of these principles inevitably converges in certain basic types of design. These types are elemental design concepts, capable of accommodating ideas of greatly diverse stamp, and responsive to flexible interpretation. The table on pages 44-45 gives to these fundamental types names descriptive of their divisional distribution and character, shows their thematic range and content, and, in a connection to be discussed later, cites examples of specific conventionalized designs or "forms" which fall under these types.

While the principles governing these fundamental distributions of ideas and localities remain constant in epoch after epoch, it is understandable in historical terms that their application in a particular period, or in accordance with a given style or aesthetic, would tend to promote characteristic conventionalizations of design. Any standardized structural procedure thus becomes *a certain form,* as for example, the "sonata-form". A form is hence merely one particular way of applying the principles of design. In reverse, a form reveals these principles as the excuse for its artistic being. Forms evolve by experimentation into a position of security through the sanction of wide use and acceptance, and are stabilized by the accumulation of masterpieces in which composers have chosen to apply the laws of design in a given way. Even so, there are individual ways displayed in the detail of the application, and no two designs based upon different musical ideas can ever be inwardly alike. Such differences may be profound, as with a classic and a romantic sonata-form, while yet the underlying organism is based on the same structural premises. Separate description and interpretation of the stated forms is not feasible here. The names of the chief ones are however given in the last double column of the table on pages 44-45; they are separated there according to their polyphonic and homophonic predilection, since the same principles of design give rise to inherently different form products in the different idioms. From the suggestion of columns 2, 3, and 4, something of the internal arrangements of these forms may also be inferred.

Still greater extent than that of the longest single design is reached by the placement of two or more separate designs in succession in some degree of relation. This is merely a more comprehensive application of the rudimentary principle of projection by addition. The individual units of such a composite are called movements and their sum a *cycle*.

Many kinds of cycle, of varied extent and diversity of interorganization, have appeared in the course of the history of music. The simpler types are based on the principle, loosely applied, of contrast by alternation, presenting movements in different degrees of slower and faster pace. Contrast of idea and mood is also brought forward with each movement within the limits of a broad relevancy. The dissociating force of constant contrast from movement to movement, and of self-contained design in each movement, is partially offset in many instances by a marked stability in locality, according to which all movements are sometimes in one tonality, or two out of three or three out of four in the main tonality.

The most sensitively organized type of cycle is based on a modified and in general relaxed application of the same principles of design which govern a single structure. That

DESIGN TYPES AND "FORMS"

NOTE:: dashes=basic divisions; letters=themes; dots=continued use of one theme; numerals=tonalities; *etc.*=may continue on the same plan; ind.=indeterminate; var.=various; dev.=developed

DESIGN TYPE	NO. OF BASIC DIVISIONS	DISTRIBUTION OF DIVISIONS, THEMES, AND CHIEF TONAL OR MODAL LOCALITIES	NO. OF BASIC THEMES OR GROUPS	EXAMPLES OF CONVENTIONALIZED "FORMS"	
				Polyphonic *	*Homophonic and Semi-polyphonic*
Unitary	1	A —— 1	1	Canon [70] Fughetta (brief type) Thru-comp.	Period Thru-comp. [20a]
Serial	Ind.	A A A *etc.* —1 —1 —1 *etc.* A A′ A″ *etc.* —1 —1 —1	1	Stanzaic Variation	Stanzaic [53] Variation [33a]

Additive	Ind.	A B C *etc.*
		—1 —1 —1
		  or or
		  2 2
			Ind.	Instrumental canzona [28]
				Thru-comp.
					Certain dances
					
					Thru-comp.

Cursive	Ind.	A B C *etc.* (A) —1 —2 —3 *etc.* 1	Ind.	Motet [43, 50] Fuga [51] Ricercare Thru-comp.	Baroque sonata movement [21a, 21b] Thru-comp. [61, 73]
	Ind.	A.......... —1 —1..........	1	Fugue [7]	

Al'ternative	2	1 2 2 1 *or* var.	1	Fugue [6]	Rondo [22]
	Ind.	A...... 1 2 2 1 *or* var.	Ind.	Rondo	Ternary [64]

Circular	3	A B A C A *etc.*
		1 2 1 3 1
		     or
		     1
			2	Ternary	Classic sonata-
					form [34a, 48]

	3	A B A
		1 2 1
		  or
		  var.
			2		

	3	A B dev. A B 1 2 var. 1 1 A............... 1 var. 1	1	Fugue [4]	
Hybrid	Ind.	Ind.	Ind.		Rondo-sonata, [12] etc.
Sui generis	Ind.	Ind.	Ind.	"Fantasy," [41] etc.	"Fantasy," etc.

* Only the divisional characteristics of polyphonic forms are brought out in this table, not their internal contrapuntal organization.

is, the cycle as a whole is drawn together by repetition and development of idea from movement to movement, by a scheme of proportions among the movements, by a balance between tonal contrast and tonal unity, and by a cumulative conception of the cyclic design as a whole. [27] This search for a comprehensive total may even proceed as far as an approximate circular unification of the cycle. The technical names of several historically important cyclic types are the suite, [8] the sonata da camera, [72] the sonata da chiesa, [21] the concerto grosso, [20] the sonata-, [13] symphony-, [34] and quartet-cycle, [46] the concerto, [11] and so forth.

The Design Contour

Superior to the factors of design which we have so far considered, there presides a still broader process, the operations of which partly exert control over the constituent processes of design, partly reflect and interpret them. This superior framework is manifested in the growing and maturing of a succession of crises distributed significantly throughout the course of a musical work. These crises are CLIMAXES, and their relations form the longest-spanned, most comprehensive coördination in design. Climax is signalized by the building up of intensities to a predestined point of emphasis, followed by release. The aesthetic formula is thus one of approach, consummation, recession. The movement of climax may be said to be analogous in the large to that which is manifested over a lesser extent in the crystallization of a tone pattern around a tone of emphasis, or in the approach of a span to its moment of completion in a cadence.

The generating of intensities may bring to bear every activity of the musical process, or it may stress selectively certain of them, in conformity to the kind and degree of climax intended. Accordingly, climax may secure intensification through a climbing of the most conspicuous pitch line. There may be a reinforced inner rhythmic activity of the ideas themselves; there may be a gradual or a rapid acceleration of the over-all pace in the approach to the moment of crisis; or there may be a combination of both of these factors, so as to secure a swifter dénouement. There is certain to be an increase in volume, which serves as an arresting reinforcement of the increased emphases in other factors of the climax. Enlarged instrumental or vocal sonority will attend augmented volume. Intensified dissonance may or may not be involved; if present, it may take the form of more tense individual combinations, or of a larger number of such combinations, or it may consist of a mixture of the two. There may also occur a spreading and filling of the texture, and added internal textural complication, as more ample room, figuratively speaking, is demanded for the pitch and time operations. Finally, there is inevitably manifested a heightened intensity in the focus and often in the complexity of the actual patterns; that is, there is greater intrinsic pressure within the design itself.

A further important aspect of the climax process is timing; for climaxes of different effect result from the relation of this factor to the other ingredients. A prolonged or a brief approach may produce merely a greater or a lesser climax respectively; or, on the contrary, a foreshortened approach, coupled with phenomenal intensities in all of the activities of the musical process, will result in a climax of extraordinary condensation. Such differences of timing are not mere exterior qualifications of the climax operation, they are an organic part of it.

While climax is in principle a line of approach to a

point of proposed intensity, it may be of artistic value to arrest the expected course of action. The cumulative movement toward the dénouement may therefore be stopped short of the goal. If it is later resumed, we have a deferred climax; if it is cut off, we have a suppressed climax. Either procedure has interesting artistic implications.

It is evident, according to the ways in which the various activities of the climax process selectively operate, that there will result different kinds and degrees of climax. Thus, within the larger design lesser climaxes unite in approach to greater ones, in confirmation of the span-within-span nature of musical design. These diversified climaxes offer different contributions, both singly and in combination, to the lining-out of the contours of the larger design. These contours are in effect a compound *climax pattern,* the progress of which constitutes the larger logic of the whole work. [2, 14, 19, 23]

There are several attributes which define the nature of the climax pattern. It involves an organized differentiation of several climaxes. Through planned spacement and timing of these climaxes, the pattern assigns meaning to the span distribution of the design. It is in the nature of the climax pattern that the succession of climaxes, whatever the local interplay of climax and anticlimax may be, shall in the large be cumulative. The climax pattern of the entire work is therefore a unity, regardless of how complex it may be. For there cannot be several equal climaxes in a single design, since they would destroy one another and disintegrate the design into several inferior though perhaps coördinate designs. It is evident that climax pattern is intrinsically based upon an asymmetrical distribution of emphases.

Every design may be said to have a climax pattern to a

48]

considerable extent unique, the arrangements of which furnish a broad view of the "expressive" progress of the work. The greater the extent of the design, the more relatively complicated its climax pattern will be, and the more individual a form it is likely to assume. It is particularly in the distinctiveness of climax curve, as well as in the ideas themselves, that different specimens of the same conventionalized form, similar in fundamental principle, differ organically from one another.

It must be noted parenthetically that points of climax consummation are not necessarily located at the ends of structural divisions. They may be; on the other hand, particularly in conjunct designs, the impact of beginning a new division, and hence of offering a new idea or a conspicuously recapitulated idea, may supply the energy for carrying the dénouement of the climax across the division line. Climax then serves as a fusing agency and as a counteractant against the separatism of sectionality in design.

Climax may finally be conceived as the function of diversified intensities, which builds up and releases the more comprehensive pressures of design, and which accordingly embraces in one cumulative movement all of the lesser functions of pressure and release which have contributed their impulses along the way.

*   *

*

The extensive design as a whole must now be viewed as the *master pattern* of all of the component patterns which we have examined. In the creative integration of these patterns, the potential interrelations of idea, locality, span, and climax are innumerable; that is, the varieties of musical design are unlimited.

But the material pattern in its entirety is not the sole and supreme pattern of music. For in the listener's combined sensuous and intellectual response to the material pattern there is etched an immaterial copattern, having no existence or final meaning except in terms of experience. This influential force in design is *mood pattern*. Entering into the formulation and projection of the ideas of every musical work, immanent in every contour of its design, there exists a predestined mood-potential: tacit until the work reaches its fulfilment in the experience of the listener, but none the less an intrinsic and calculable factor in its design.

Music, as a time art, is inherently a lyric art. It requires an appreciable range of time, both to shape its tone patterns into intelligible idea and to evoke the salient mood. The first process in mood patterning is hence the *definition* of an initial mood through sufficient prolongation to produce a lyric concentration. [18, 59] This is essentially the function of statement or exposition of mood and analogous to, although not necessarily exactly coincident with the statement of thematic idea. Following the statement of mood, the mood pattern advances, as does the material pattern, by means of the functions of mood development and restatement; in the case of mood pattern, the former process greatly predominates over the latter.

Mood development may proceed by various degrees and kinds of change. The stated mood, as it is progressively maintained, may be subjected to an *inflection,* [23] which turns its effect in a subtly modified direction without loss of continuity or homogeneity. Inflection carried farther results in *subdivision* of mood, [17a] in which a mood generality is broken down into sharpened aspects of itself, the individuality of which may be so strengthened by prolongation that new and even independent mood phases are created in the pattern. Such subdivision, far from undermining the broader mood of origin, tends to enhance it. A mood and its phases may thus be drawn by development into a homogeneously *blended succession* of moods. [73]

The process of mood development of itself introduces the function of *contrast* into the mood pattern. If the development is sufficiently prolonged, or if it moves rapidly, marked contrasts of mood are brought into comparison at whatever closeness of range the development determines. But more directly potent effects of contrast may be secured by the juxtaposition and hence the immediate comparison of different moods in a planned relation. [66] The contrast may lie within a frame of clearly assimilable relation, or it may be so sharp as to constitute an actual interruption of the larger mood continuity of the passage. Such intense assertions as the latter are *rhetorical* in character, [1, 16, 69] and by their vividness produce points of emphasis in the mood pattern, which must be regulated in strength and frequency to the interests of that pattern as a whole. Rhetorical effects are of course associated with specific devices in the patterns of the ideas themselves; and these patterns are correspondingly subjected to the interruption of their normal course. After a rhetorical intrusion the mood which has been invaded may be resumed, or, by a more delicately balanced process, a new orientation in mood may be made to grow out of the intrusion without damage to the consistency of the larger plan.

In the operations of mood contrast important conditions involved are those of amount and variety of contrast, and rate and frequency of change. As with any other form of pattern, the qualitative principle of balanced forces of

[51

mood contrast obtains; at the same time a quantitative distribution of mood spans according aesthetically convincing proportions in the scheme of the whole must be assured. For multiplicity of mood effect, induced by development and contrast, must in the nature of the case bear a suitable relation to the extent of the composition. But however great the extent or diverse the mood content of a work may be, if it is to contain itself as an aesthetically satisfactory whole, it must secure, in the processes of mood development and contrast, a palpable over-all mood as the common denominator and focus of its constituent moods. [73, 68] Many a work well planned in formula falls apart for lack of this broader mood synthesis.

In the actual projection of a work of considerable extent, the combined principles of statement, of development by inflection, subdivision, and blended succession, and of contrast, will in one way or another manifest themselves. Through their interplay and mutual support the mood pattern acquires flexibility and range, and achieves its intimate coördination with the climax pattern of the design. It is, in fact, through the coöperation of the climax scheme that the mood pattern receives its most objective and tangible delineation. As is true of all other aspects of musical pattern, mood pattern is cumulative in nature and so symbolizes the larger lyric continuity, which is the essence of music itself.

A pattern of mood effects thus awaits release in every phase of musical design, from the theme, as it takes form in the first motive, to the far-flung contour of the climax pattern of the work as a whole. It is upon the distinctiveness of this mood pattern, as much as upon the quality of the ideas and the conviction of the design, that the individuality of a work rests. The mood pattern is the most subtle index of the music's personality, transcending and embracing all its other traits. The envisioned mood pattern hence becomes the primordial motivation of the musical organism, — the emotional experience of the composer, in readiness to be transmuted into that of the listener. Music is accordingly both mood-motivated pattern and pattern-evoked mood.

Musical design may consequently not be viewed as a mechanistic abstraction, a self-contained, detached, geometric unreality. It is rather the projection of mood into the realm of tone relations. The two — design and mood — are one, inseparable, merely different aspects of the same thing. That thing is the "expressively" integrated work of musical art itself, as it lives in the experience of the listener.

LISTENING REPERTORY

Bracketed numerals in the text refer to the correspondingly numbered musical illustrations given in the following LISTENING REPERTORY *of phonograph records. It is obvious that each illustration actually exhibits more characteristics than the particular one for which it is cited, and that the illustrations overlap one another. Records belonging to sets or collections, but which are in most cases obtainable separately, are marked with an asterisk.*

The illustrations represent a galaxy of important composers and form a very brief anthology of music literature.

1   BACH, CARL PHILIPP EMANUEL (1714-1788), Sonata, F minor, I. Allegro assai*

2   BACH, JOHANN SEBASTIAN (1685-1750), Fantasie, G minor, for organ, ("Great")

3   —, Fugue, C sharp minor (Das wohltemperierte Klavier, bk. 1, no. 4)

4   —, Fugue, G minor (op. cit., bk. 1, no. 16)

5   —, Fugue, B minor (op. cit., bk. 1, no. 24) *

6   —, Fugue, C minor (op. cit., bk. 2, no. 2) *

7   —, Fugue, E major (op. cit., bk. 2, no. 9) *

8   —, Suite no. 6, D minor, ("English")

8a   — —, II. Allemande*

9   —, Wachet auf, for organ, (chorale-prelude, Schübler no. 1)

10   BARTÓK, BÉLA (1881-), Quartet no. 2, op. 17, for strings, I. Moderato*

11   BEETHOVEN, LUDWIG VAN (1770-1827), Concerto no. 5, E flat major, op. 73, for pianoforte and orchestra, ("Emperor")

12   —, Sonata, C minor, op. 13, ("Pathétique"), IV. Rondo: Allegro*

13   —, Sonata appassionata, F minor, op. 57

14   —, Symphony no. 3, E flat major, op. 67, ("Eroica"), I. Allegro con brio*

14a   — —, II. Marcia funebre: Adagio assai*

[55

54 PURCELL, HENRY (1658-1695), Dido and Aeneas, "When I am laid in Earth", act 3, (no. 37)
55 RAMEAU, JEAN PHILIPPE (1683-1764), Castor et Pollux, "Tristes apprêts", (Air de Télaïre), act 2, sc. 2
56 SCARLATTI, ALESSANDRO (1659-1725), O cessate di piagarmi, (arietta)
57 SCARLATTI, DOMENICO (1685-1757), Toccata, L.422
58 SCHÖNBERG, ARNOLD (1874-   ), Klavierstück, op. 11, no. 2
59 SCHUBERT, FRANZ (1797-1828), Am Meer, (Schwanengesang no. 12)
60 —, Symphony, B minor, ("Unfinished"), 1. Allegro moderato*
61 —, Der Wanderer, op. 4, no. 1
62 SCHÜTZ, HEINRICH (1585-1672), Ich bin ein rechter Weinstock, (motet)
63 SCHUMANN, ROBERT (1810-1856), Bittendes Kind, op. 15, no. 4, (Kinderscenen)
64 —, Carnaval, op. 9, Valse allemande (no. 16) *
65 —, Des Abends, op. 11, no. 1, (Fantasiestücke)
66 —, Phantasie, C major, op. 17, 1. Allegro molto appassionato*
67 SIBELIUS, JEAN (1865-   ), Symphony no. 7, C major, op. 105
68 STRAUSS, RICHARD (1864-   ), Till Eulenspiegels lustige Streiche, op. 28
69 STRAVINSKY, IGOR (1882-   ), Le Sacre du Printemps
70 Sumer is icumen in (c.1240) (On Columbia record D-40119 the melody is sung separately before the canon begins) *
71 Troubadour, Kalenda maya (c.1195) (Raimbaut de Vaqueiras) *
72 VIVALDI, ANTONIO (c.1680-1743), Sonata da camera, G minor, for 2 violins, viola da gamba, continuo (harpsichord)
73 WAGNER, RICHARD (1813-1883), Die Götterdämmerung, Siegfrieds Tod, act 3, sc. 2
74 —, Die Meistersinger, Vorspiel
75 — —, "Morgenlich leuchtend", (Walthers Preislied), act 3, sc. 5
76 —, Tristan und Isolde, Vorspiel

Copies of THE PATTERN OF MUSIC *may be
ordered through your bookstore, or obtained
from* THE VASSAR COOPERATIVE BOOKSHOP,
VASSAR COLLEGE, POUGHKEEPSIE, NEW YORK.
The price is ninety-five cents.

Printed in U. S. A.